My Fantasy
Angela Spugnardi

Copyright © 2018 Angela Spugnardi

All rights reserved.

ISBN:1986025853
ISBN-13:978-1986025850

To my brave boy,
who once was blind and now sees only the beauty in everything.

A WORD FROM THE ARTIST

My world is chaotic, my camera steadies my hand. When all hope is fading, I retreat into my art, using my lens to fill my daydreams with the fantasy I wish was my reality.

The world is never what we wish, but within the growing madness there is still beauty. Look closely, it is all around you...

Angela Spugnardi

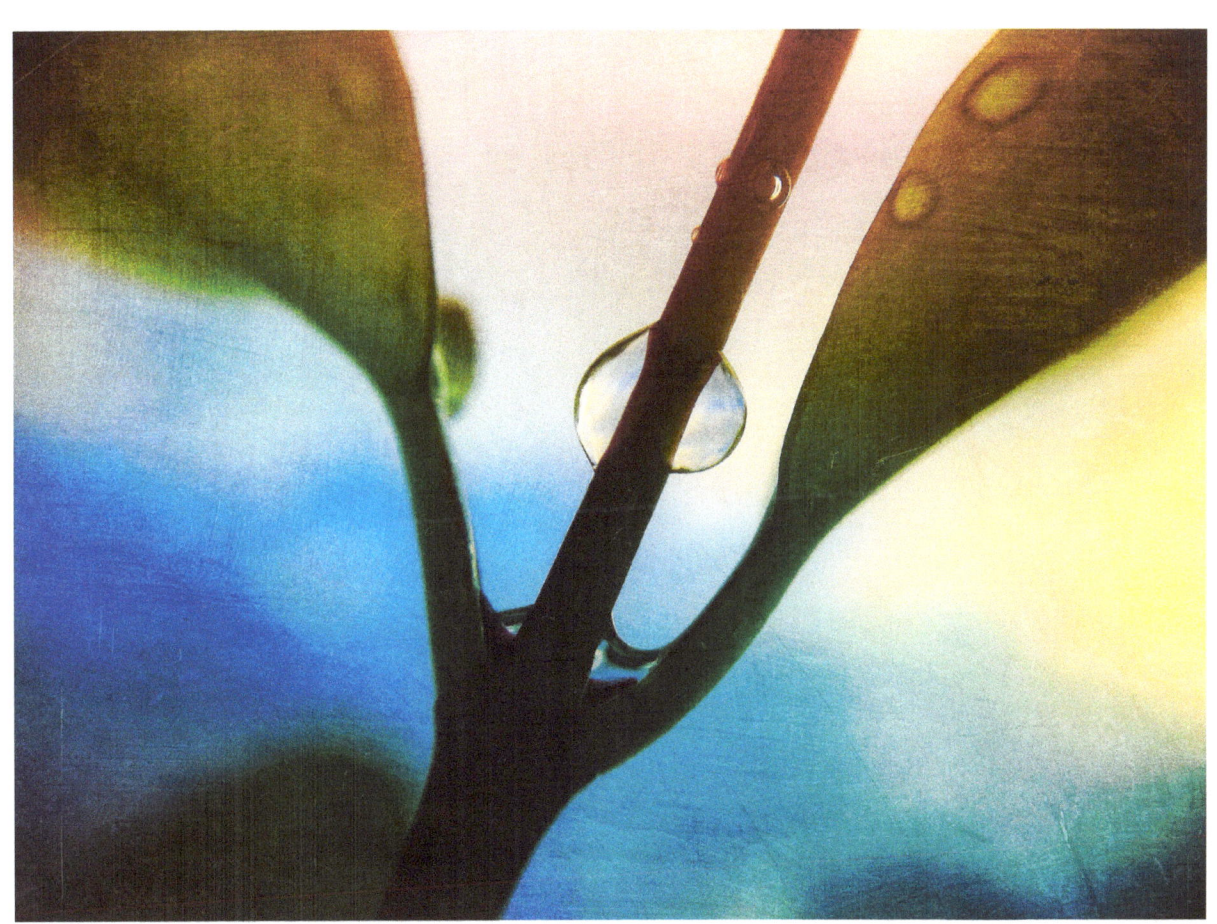

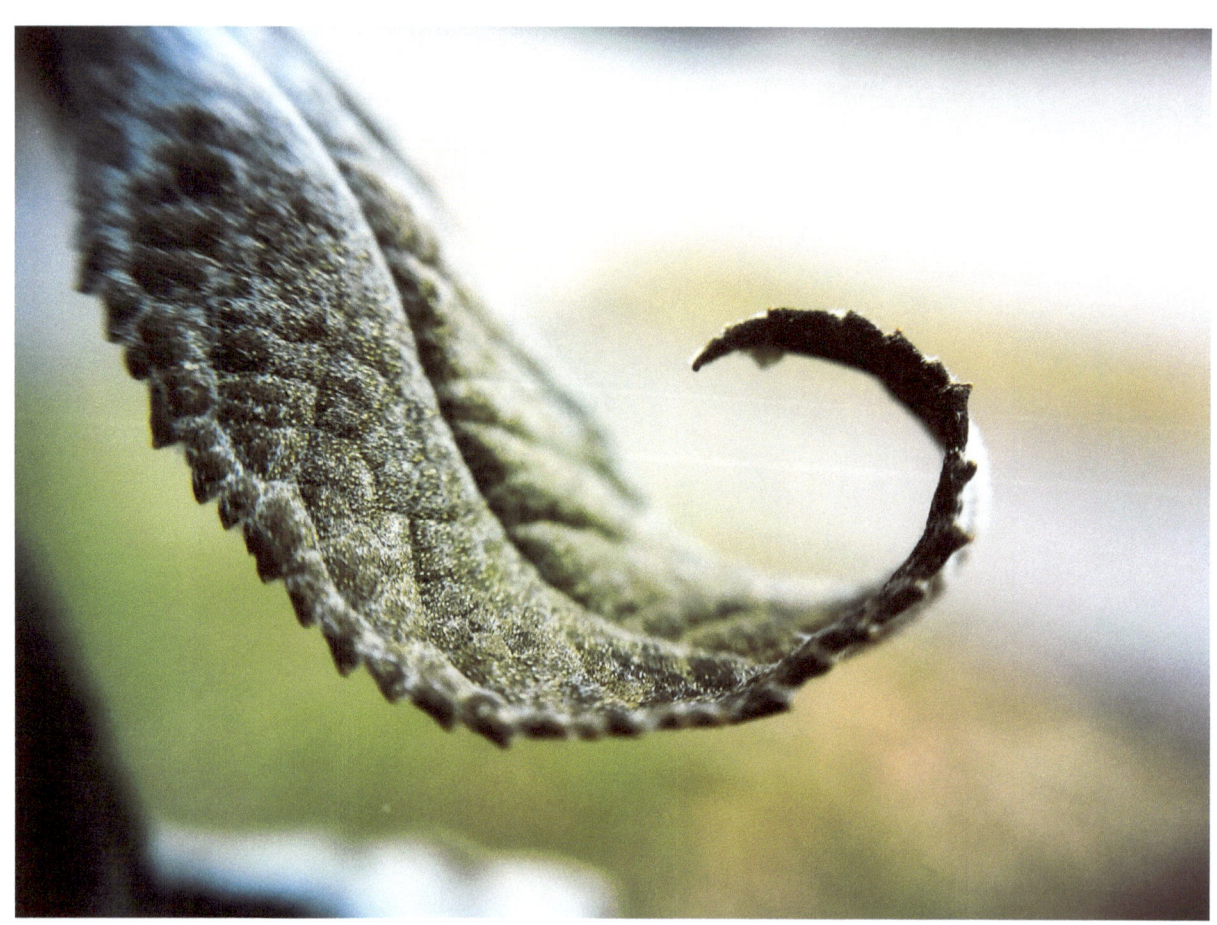

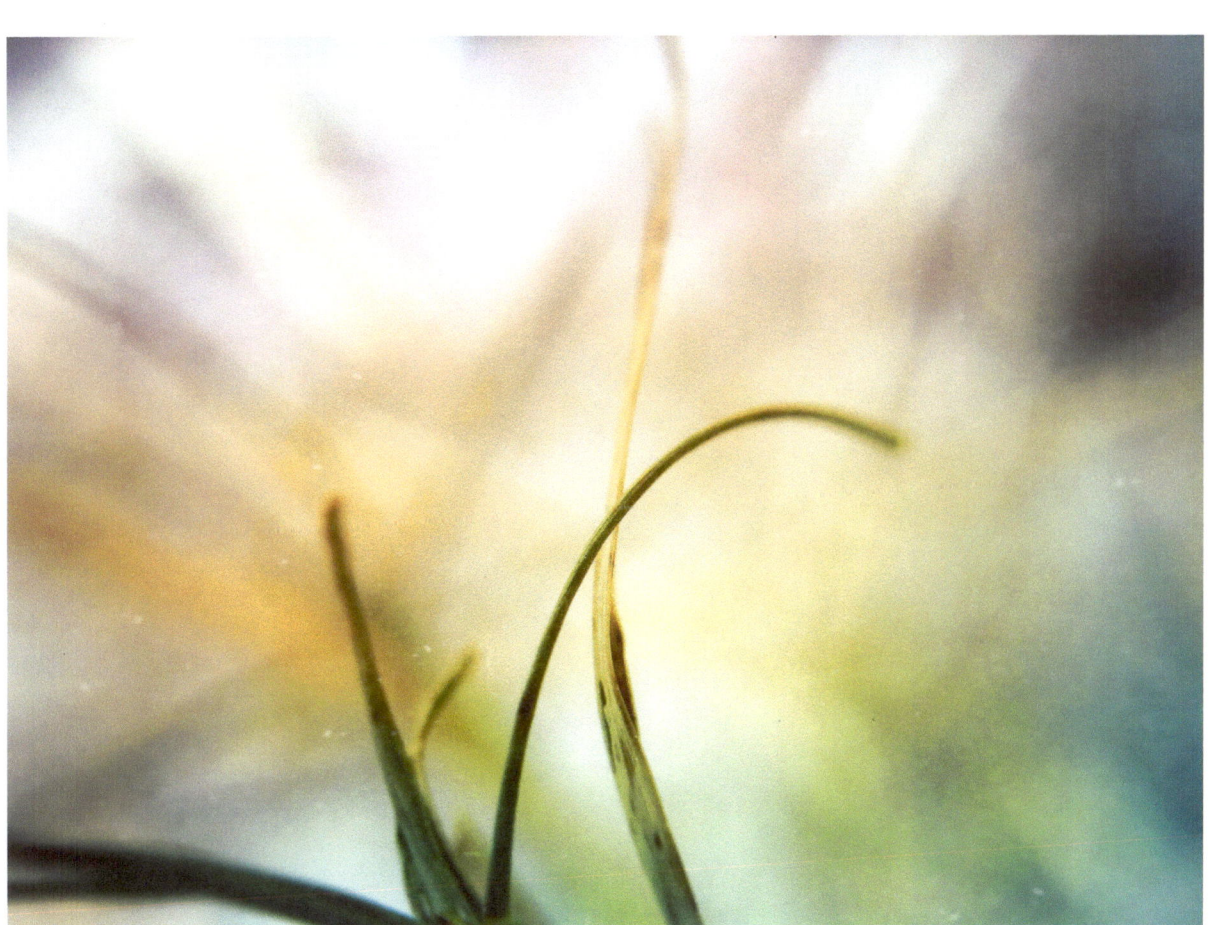

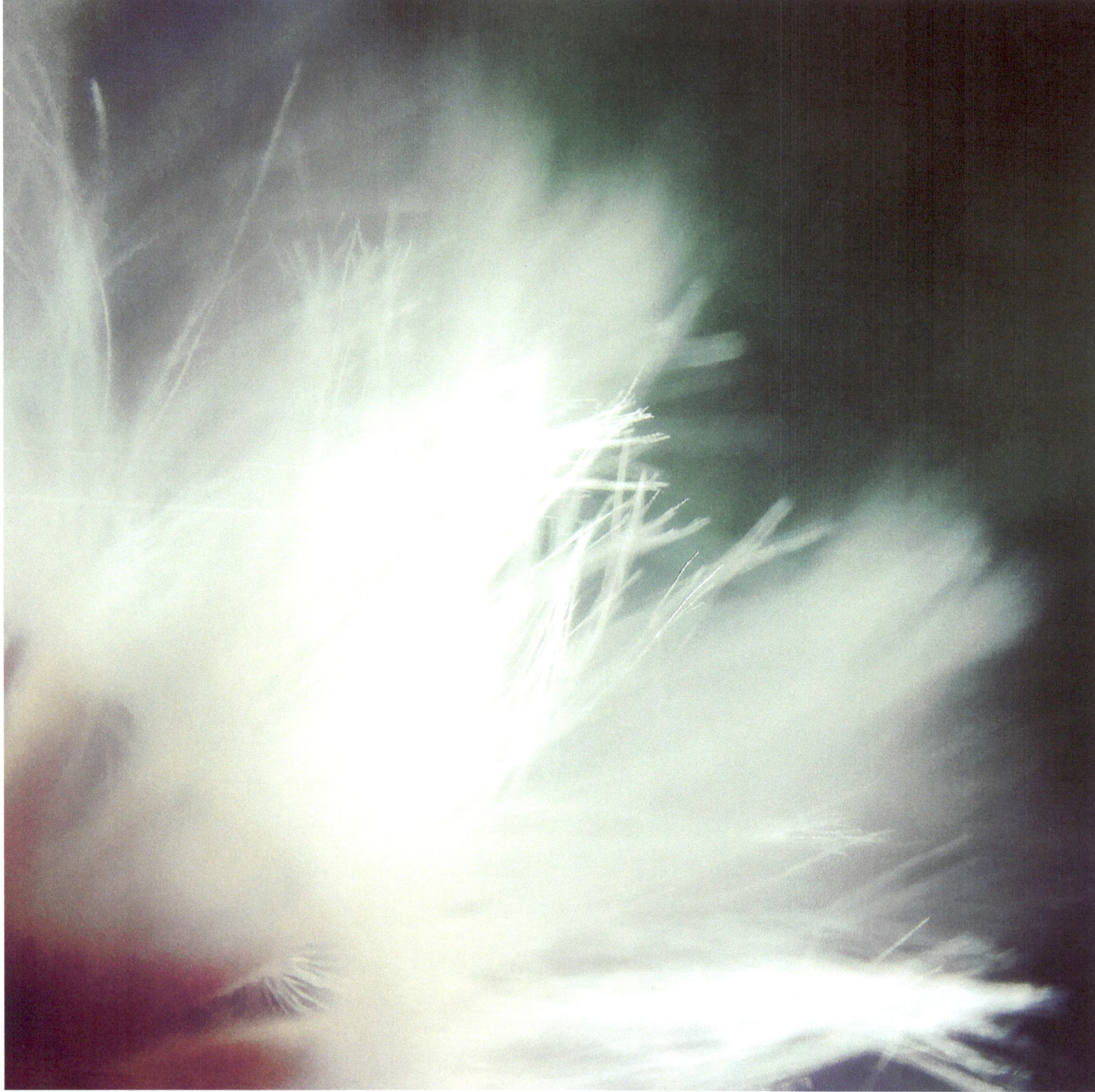

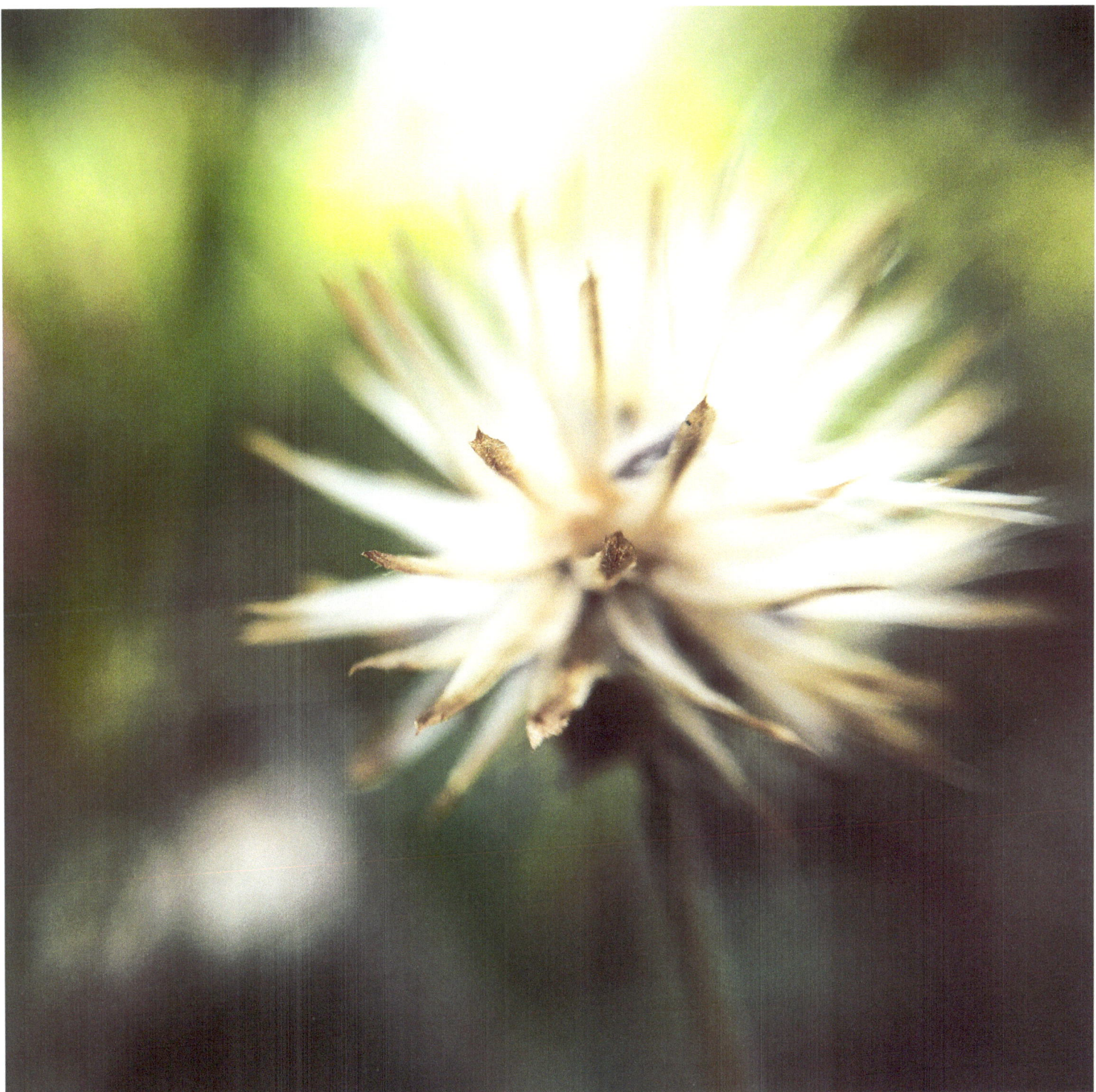

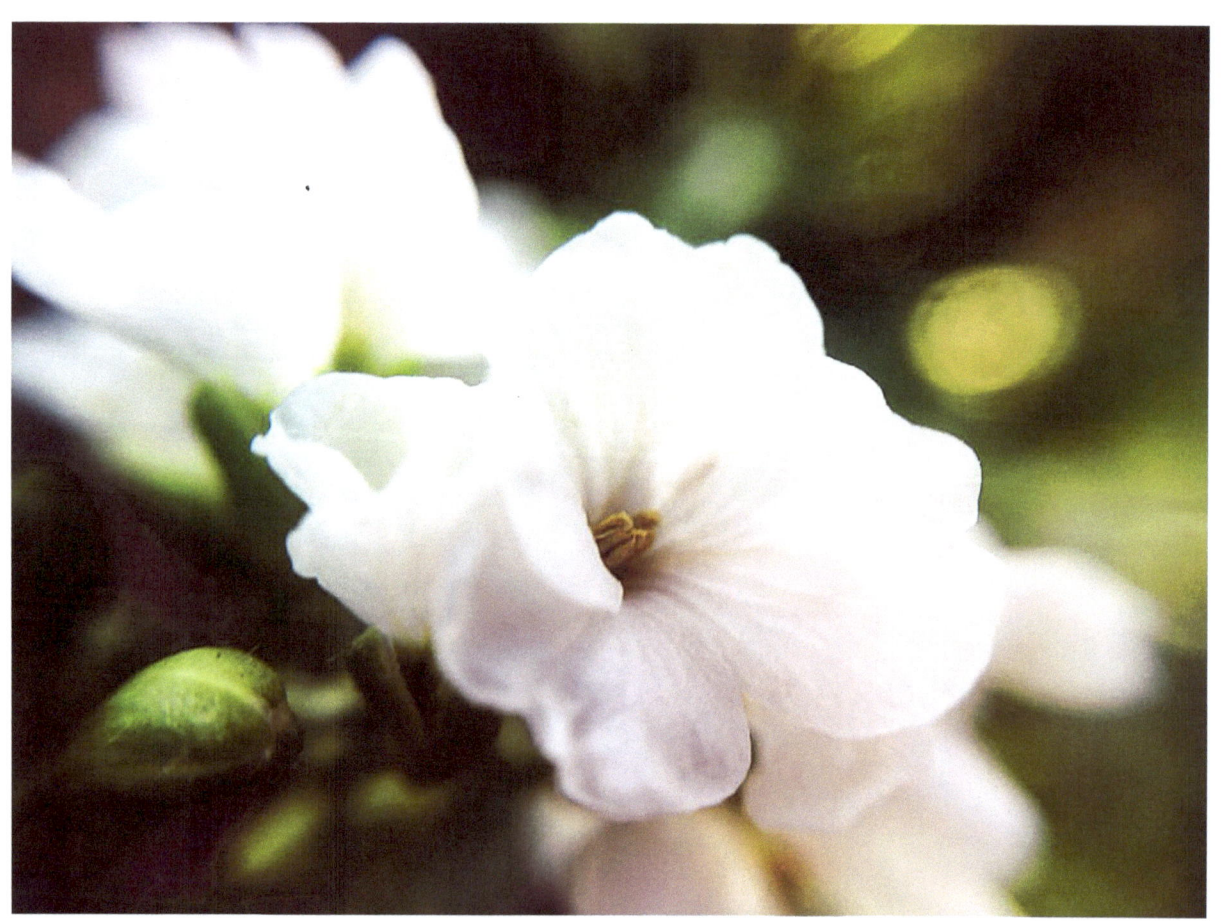

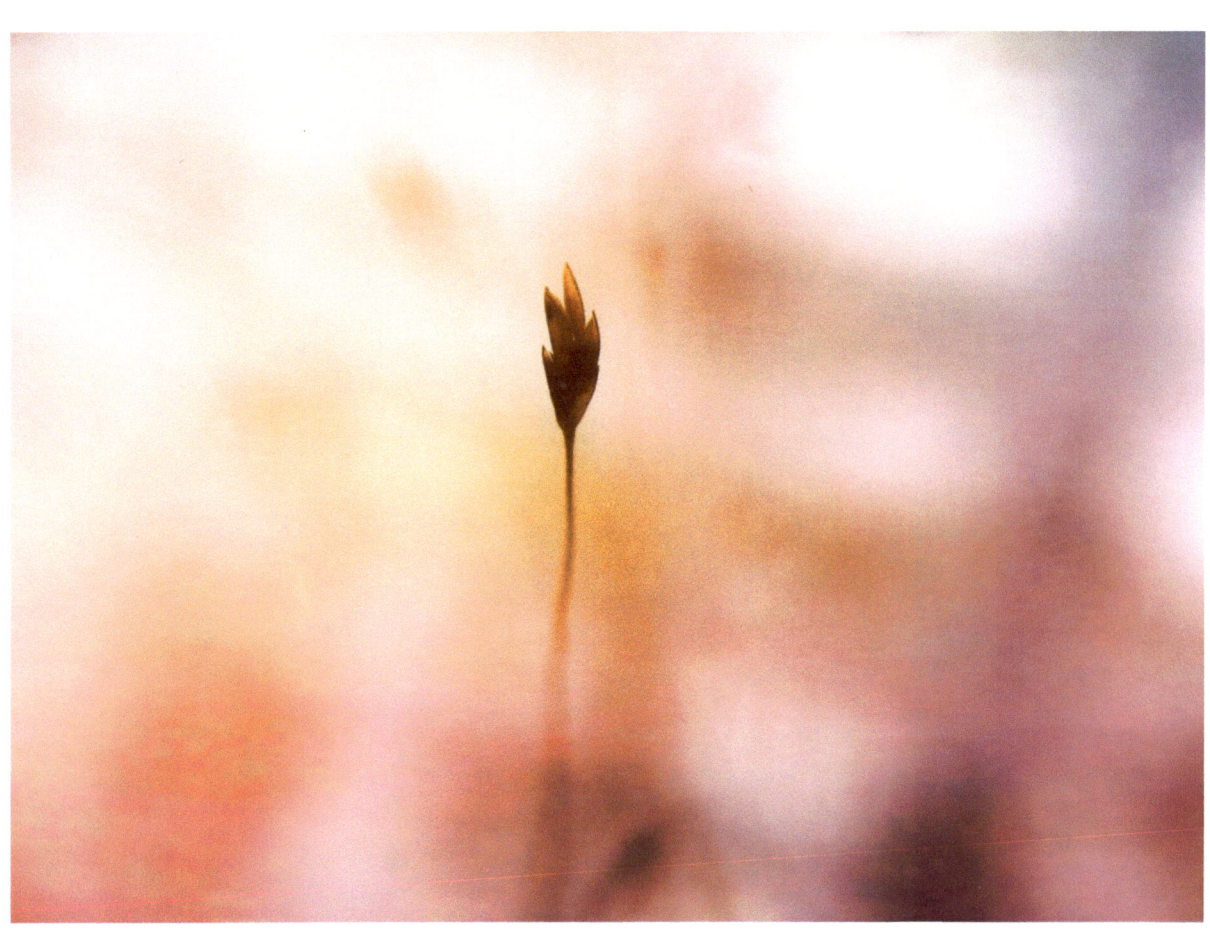

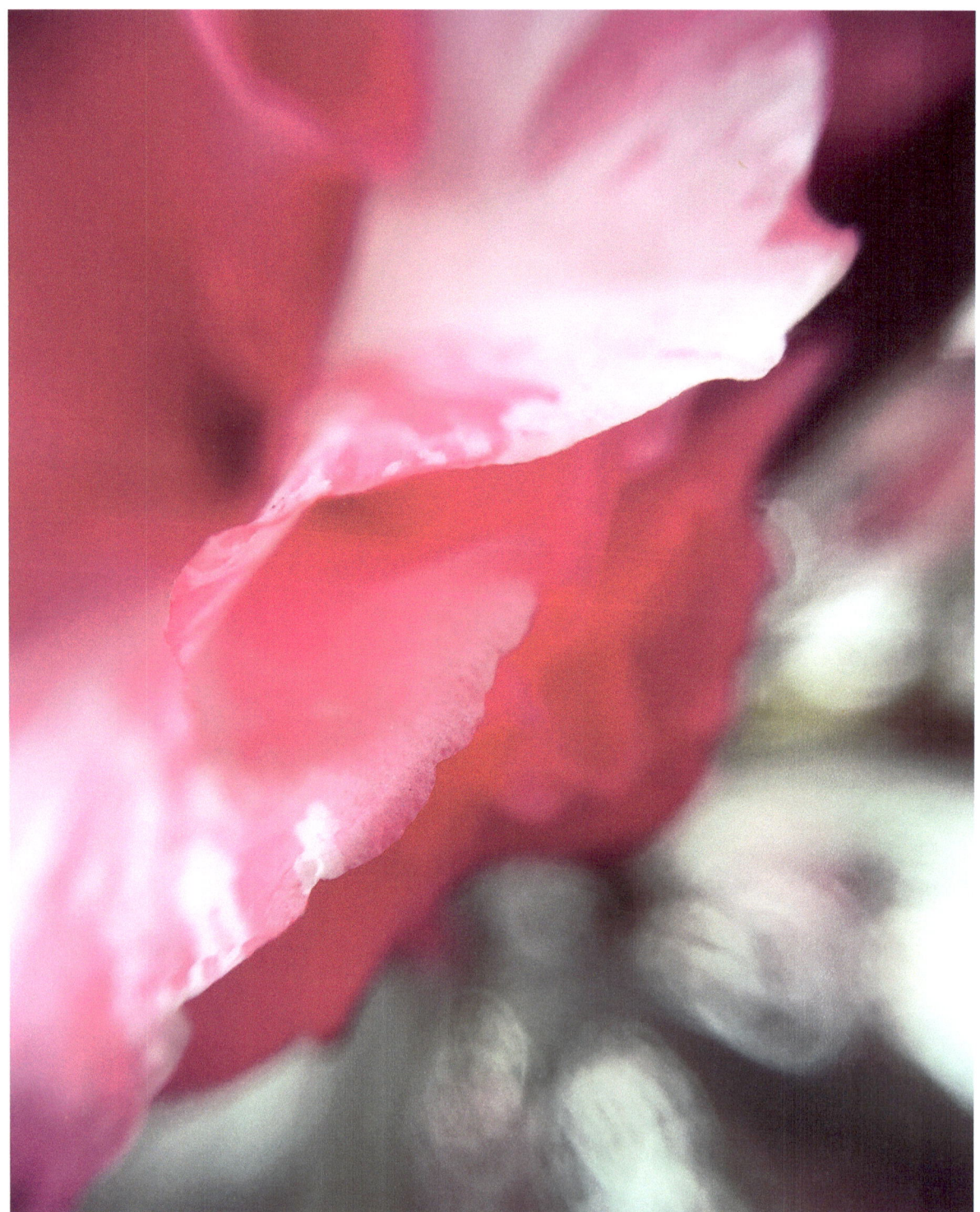

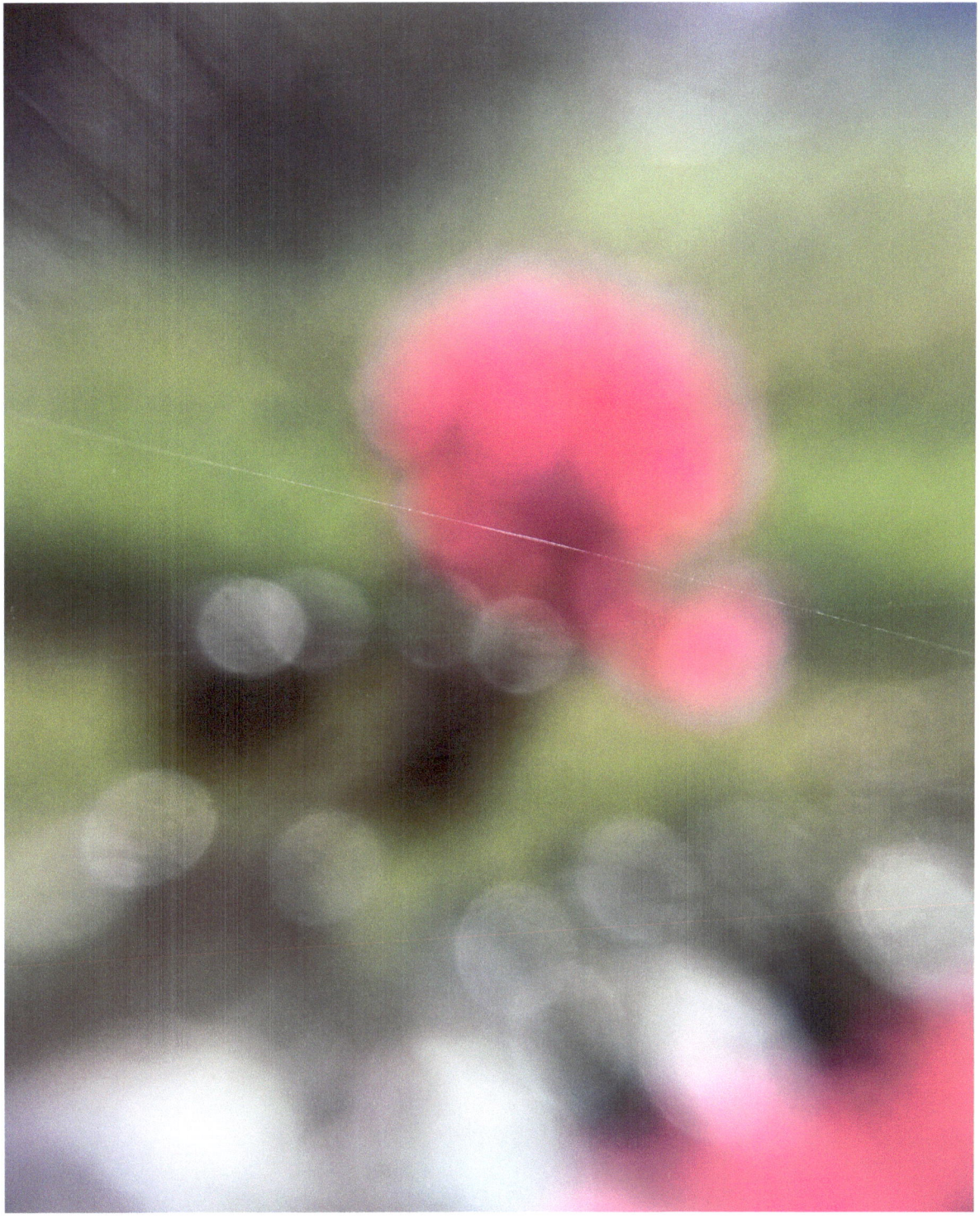

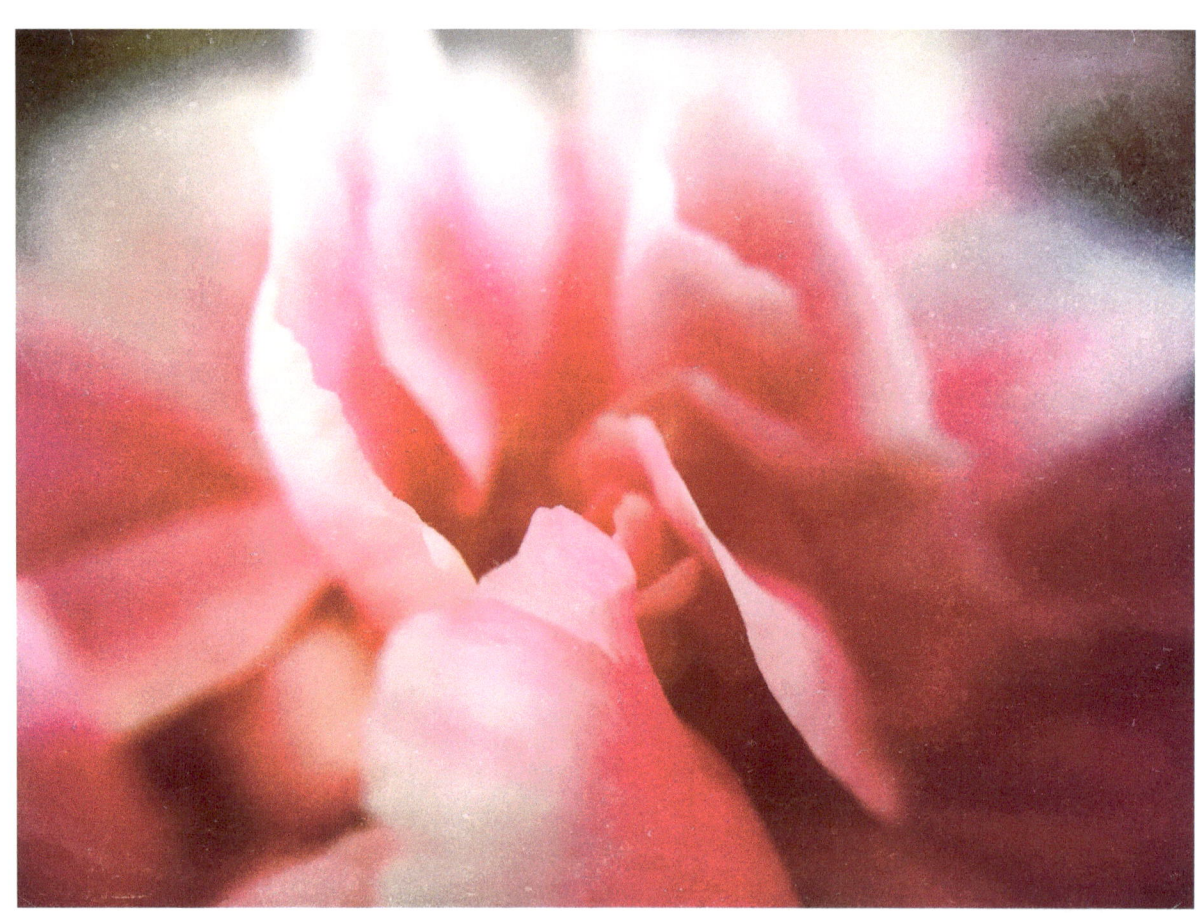

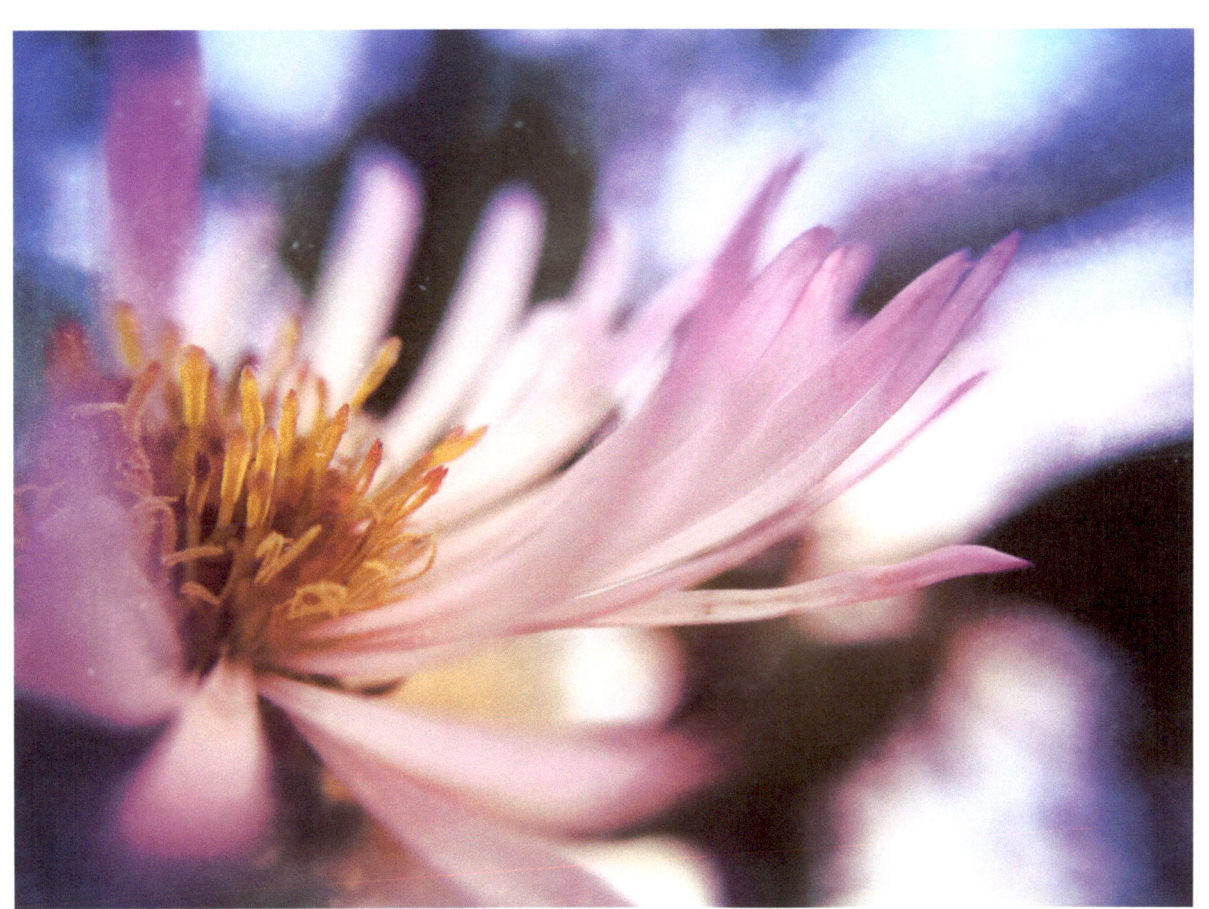

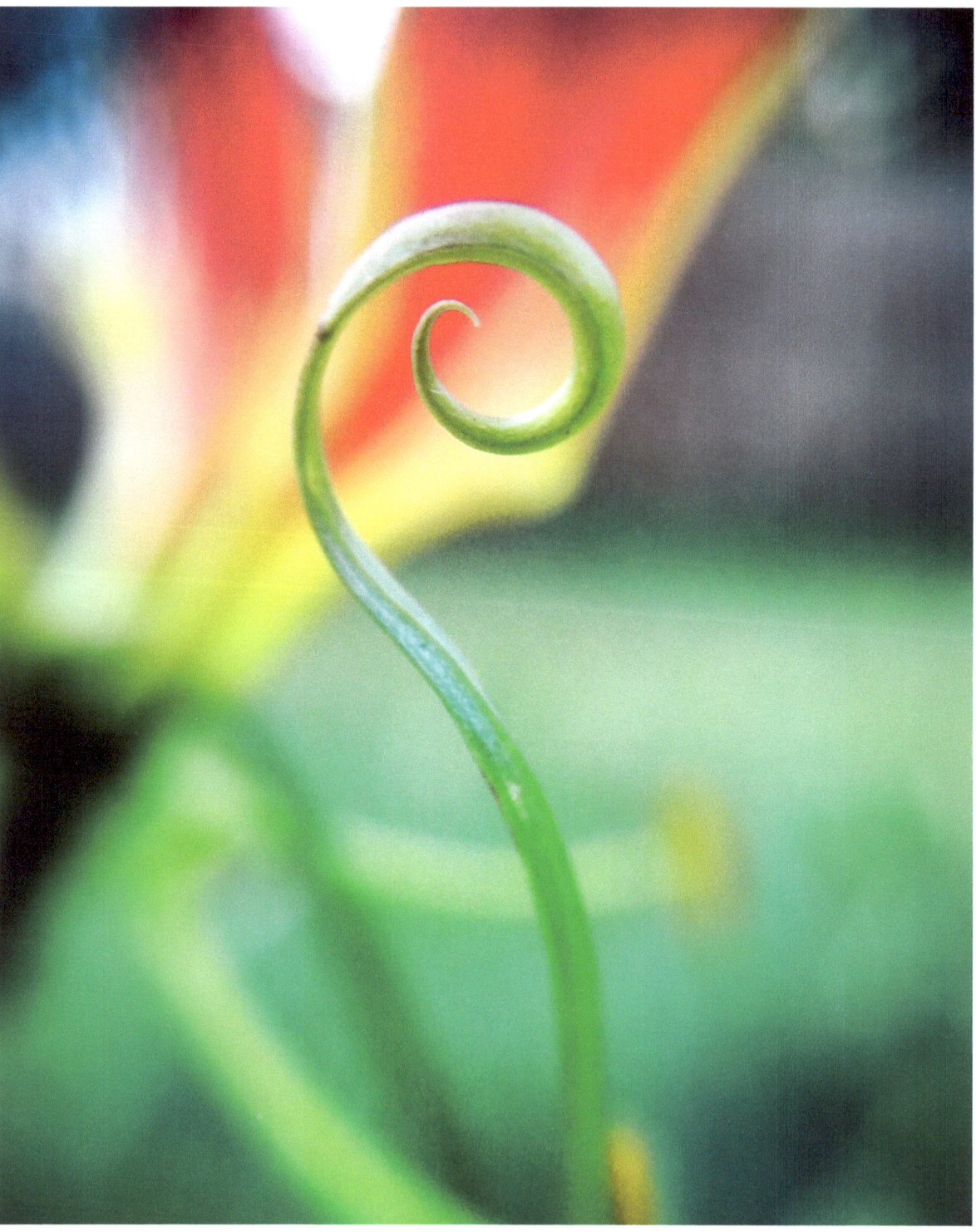

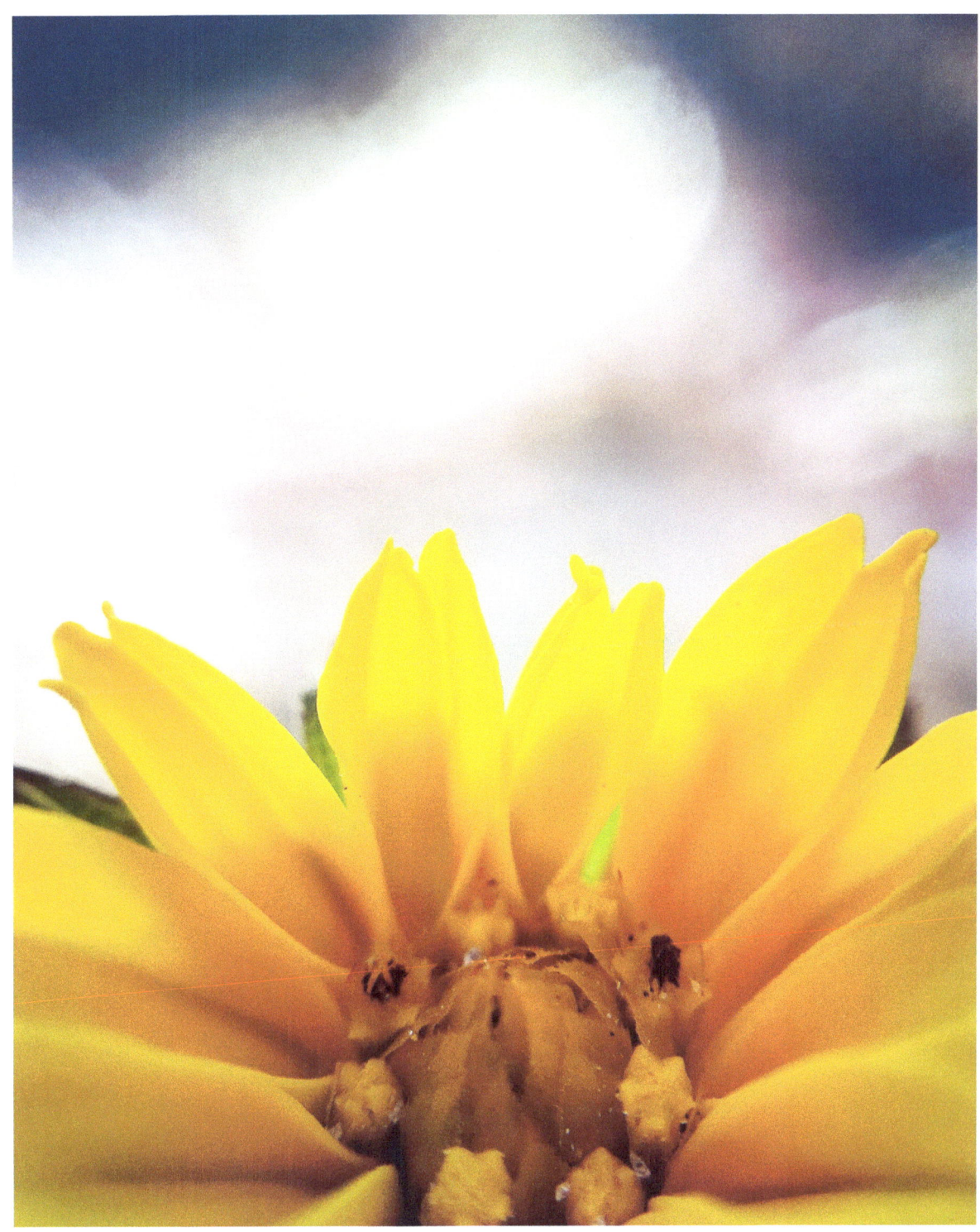

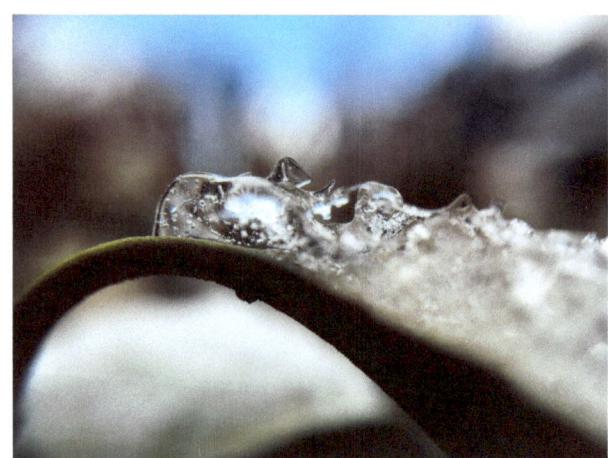
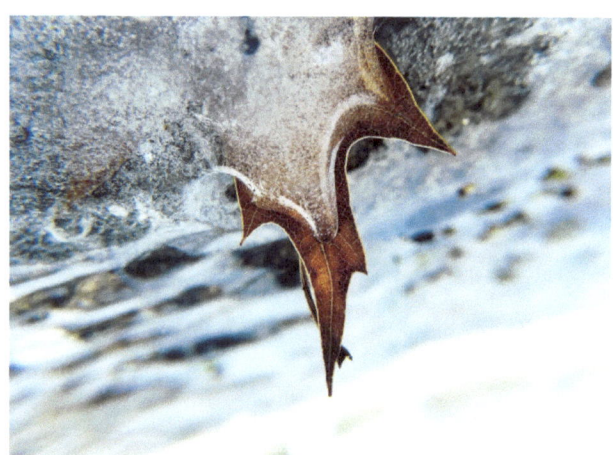
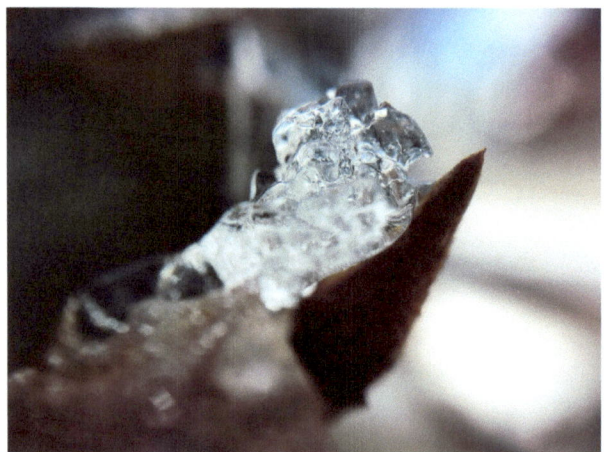
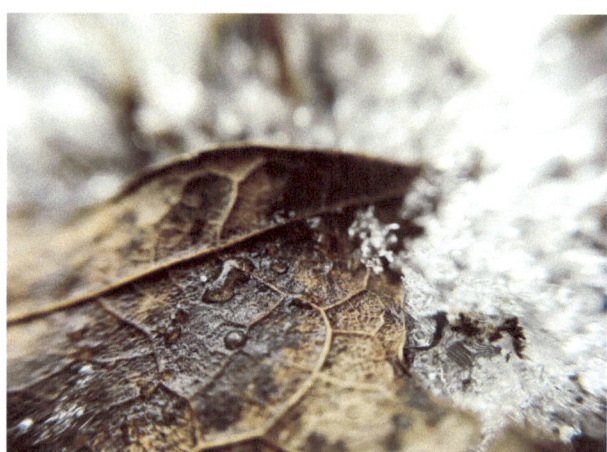

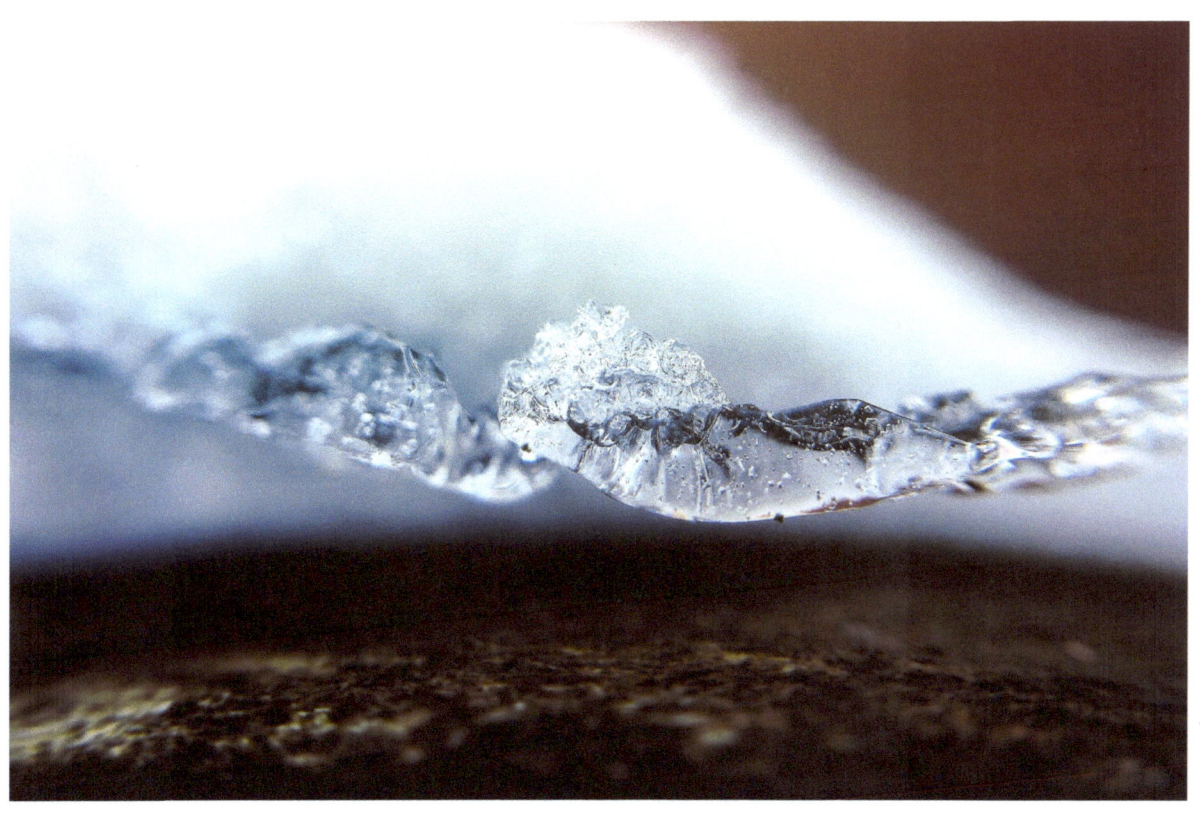

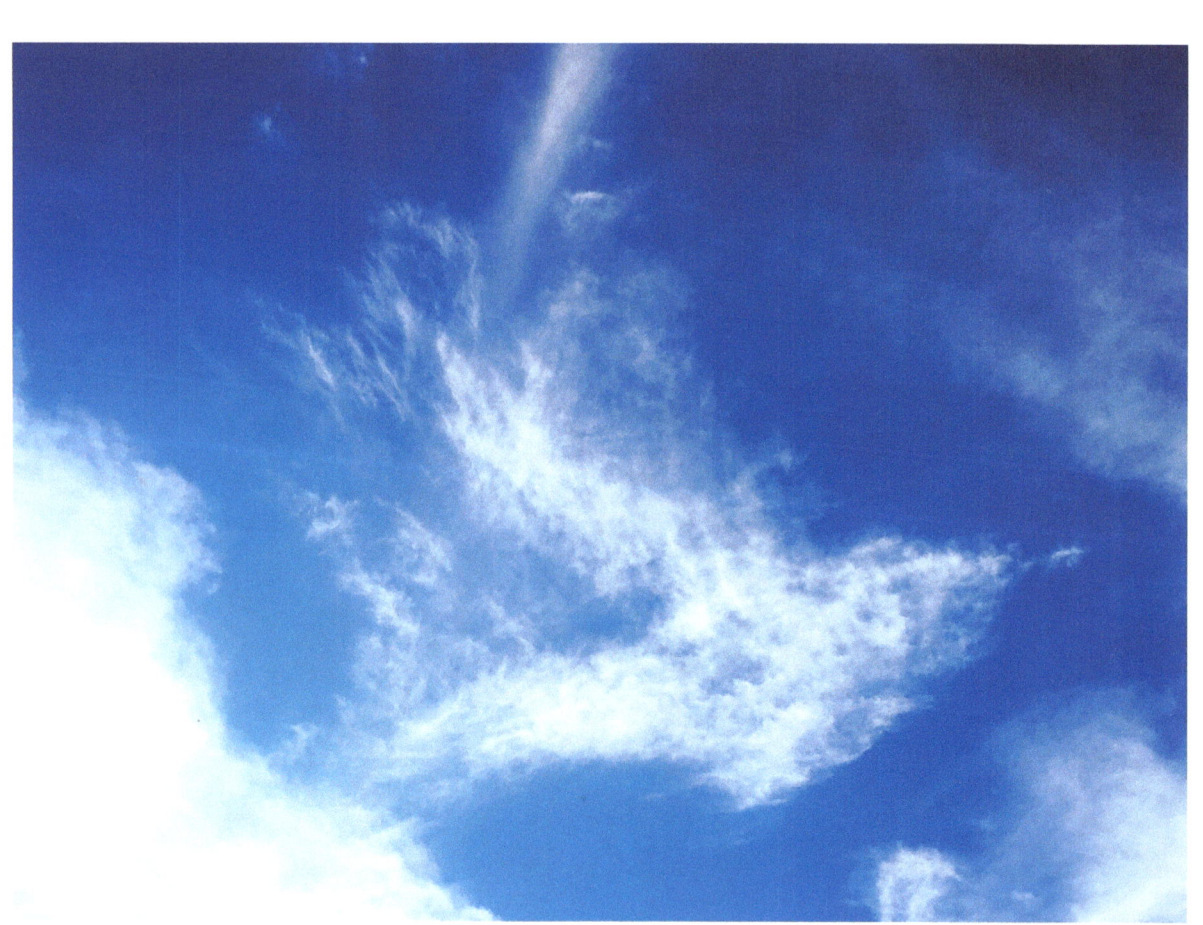

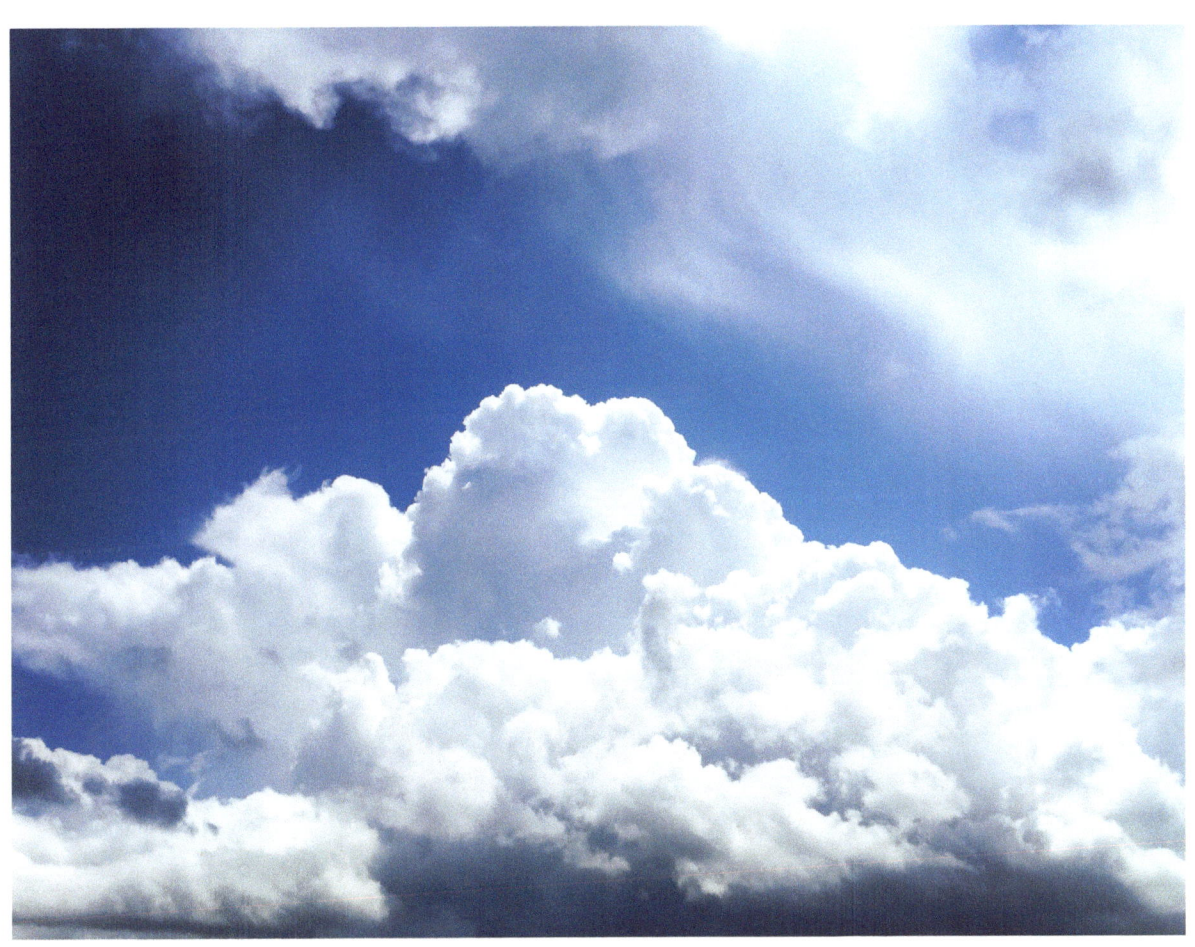

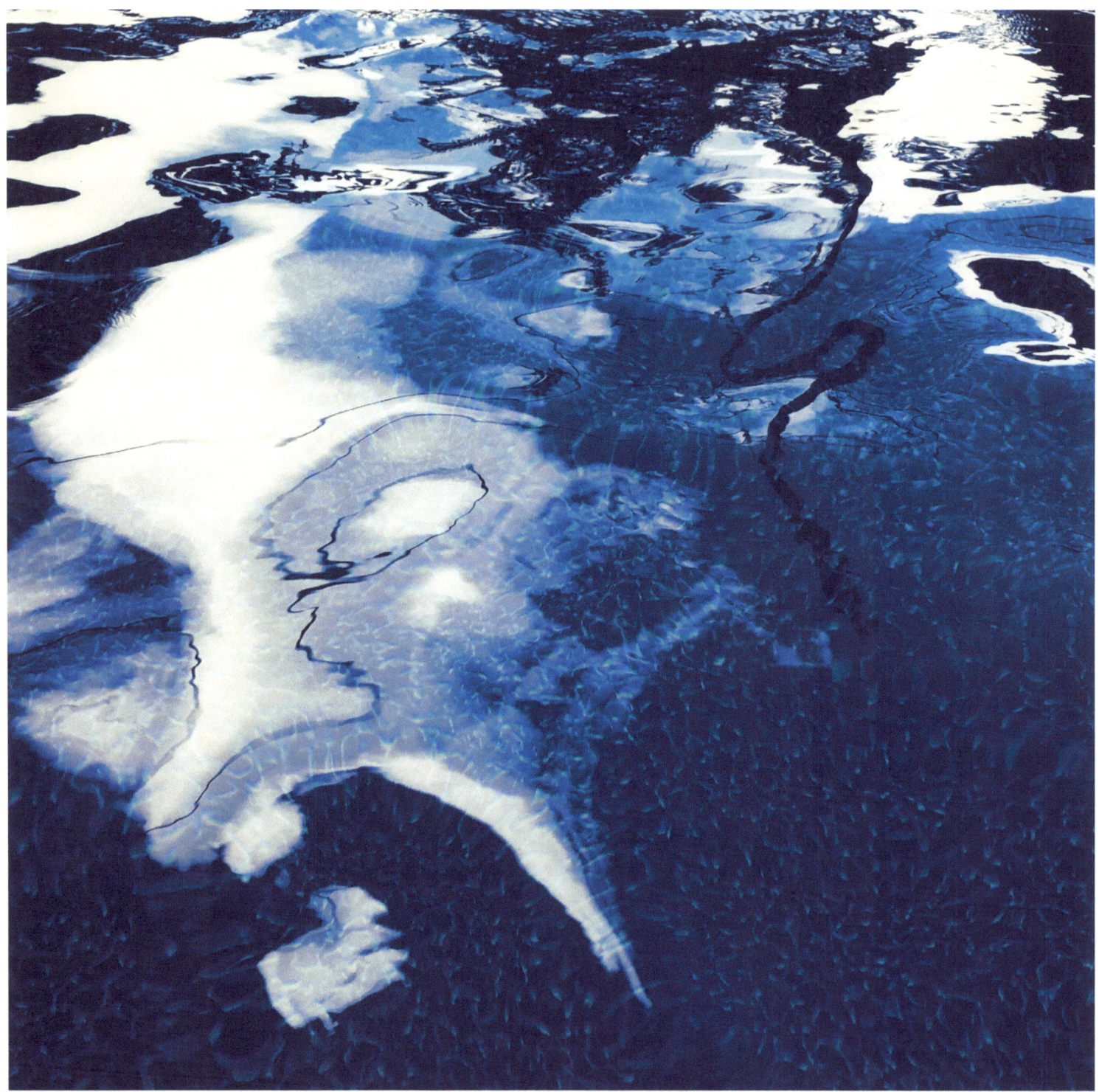

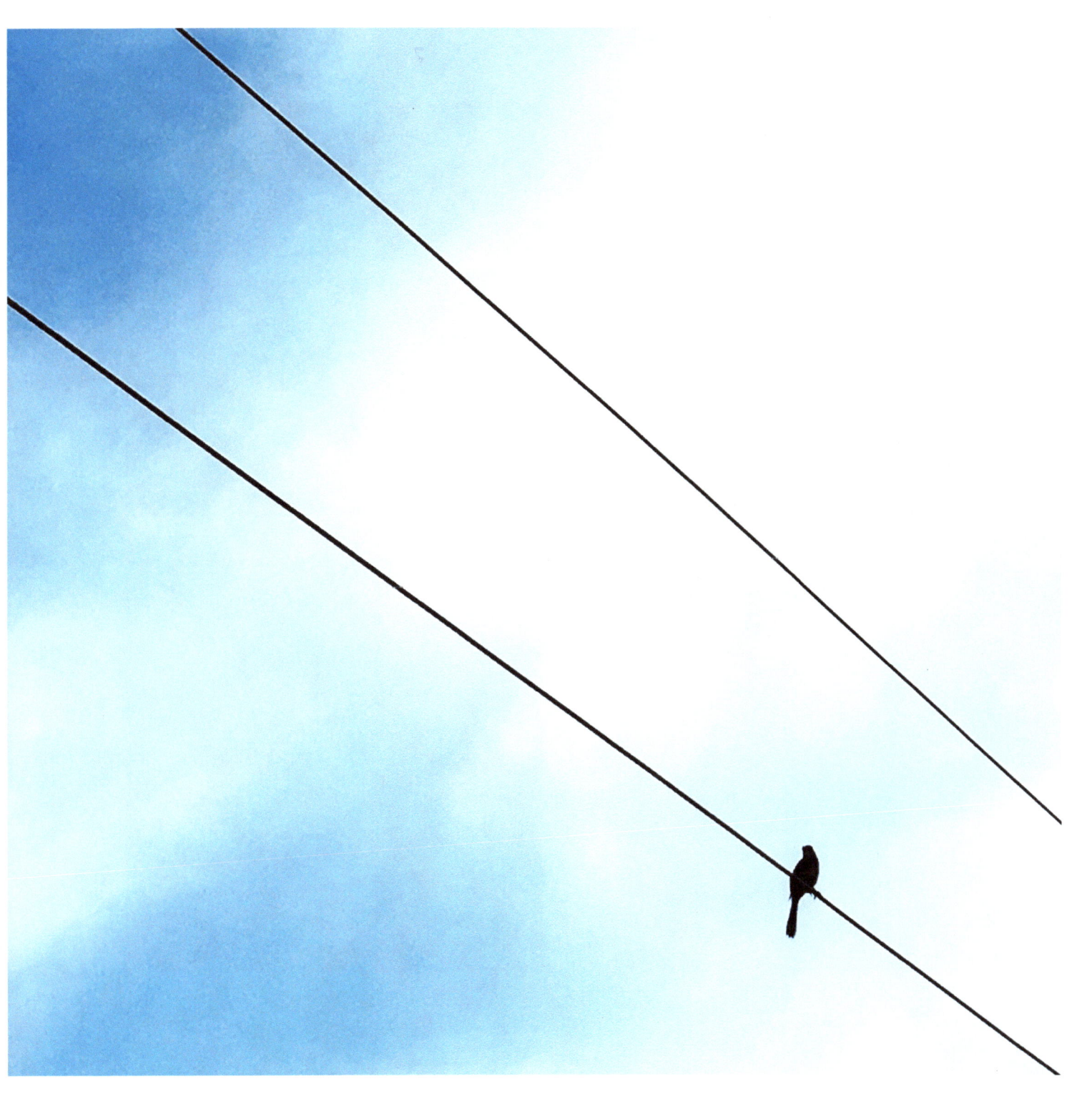

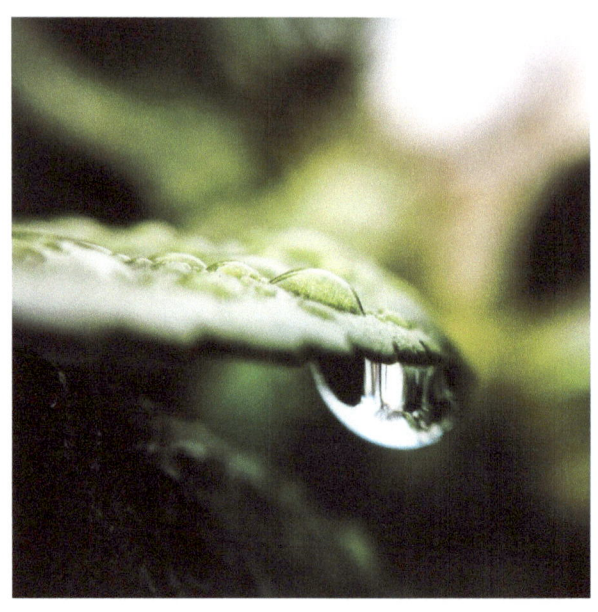
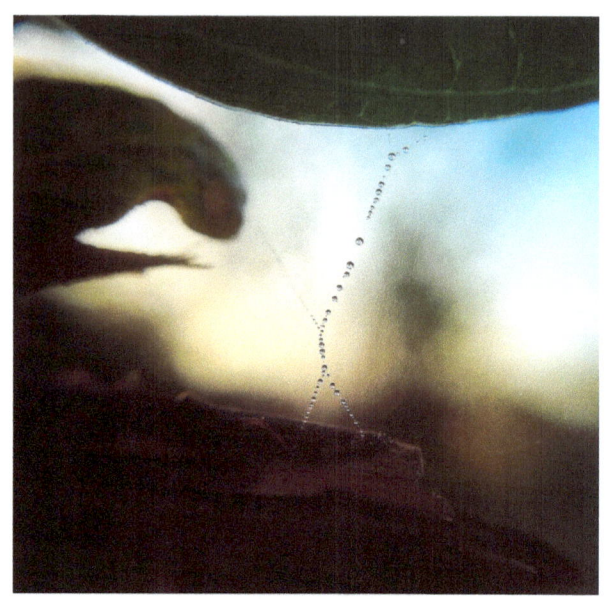
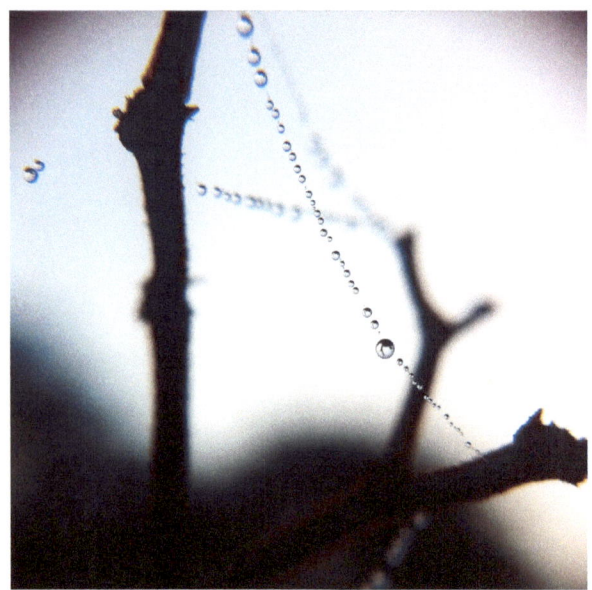
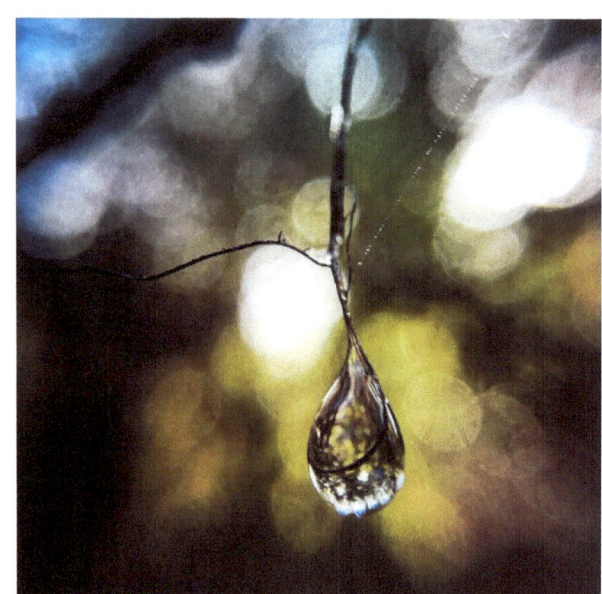

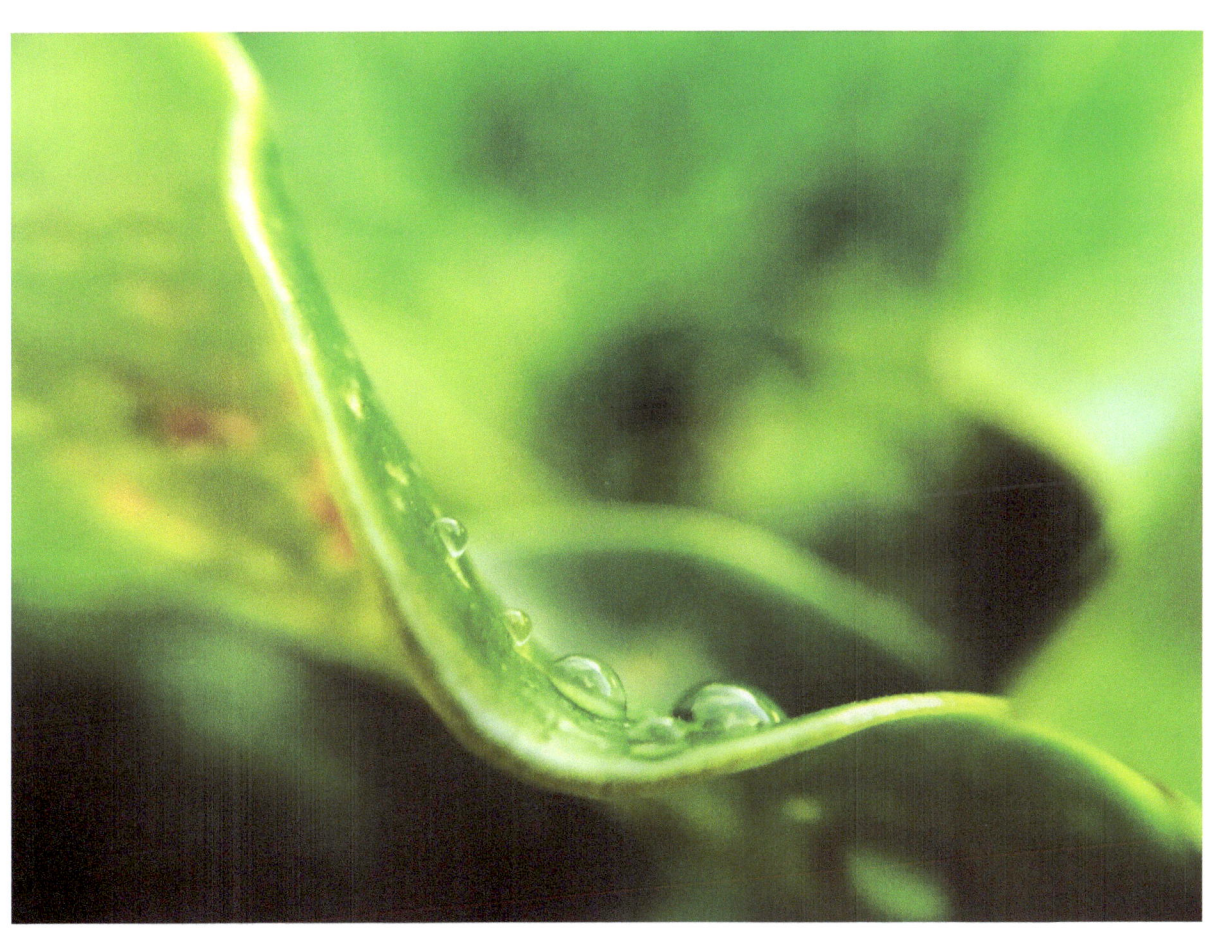

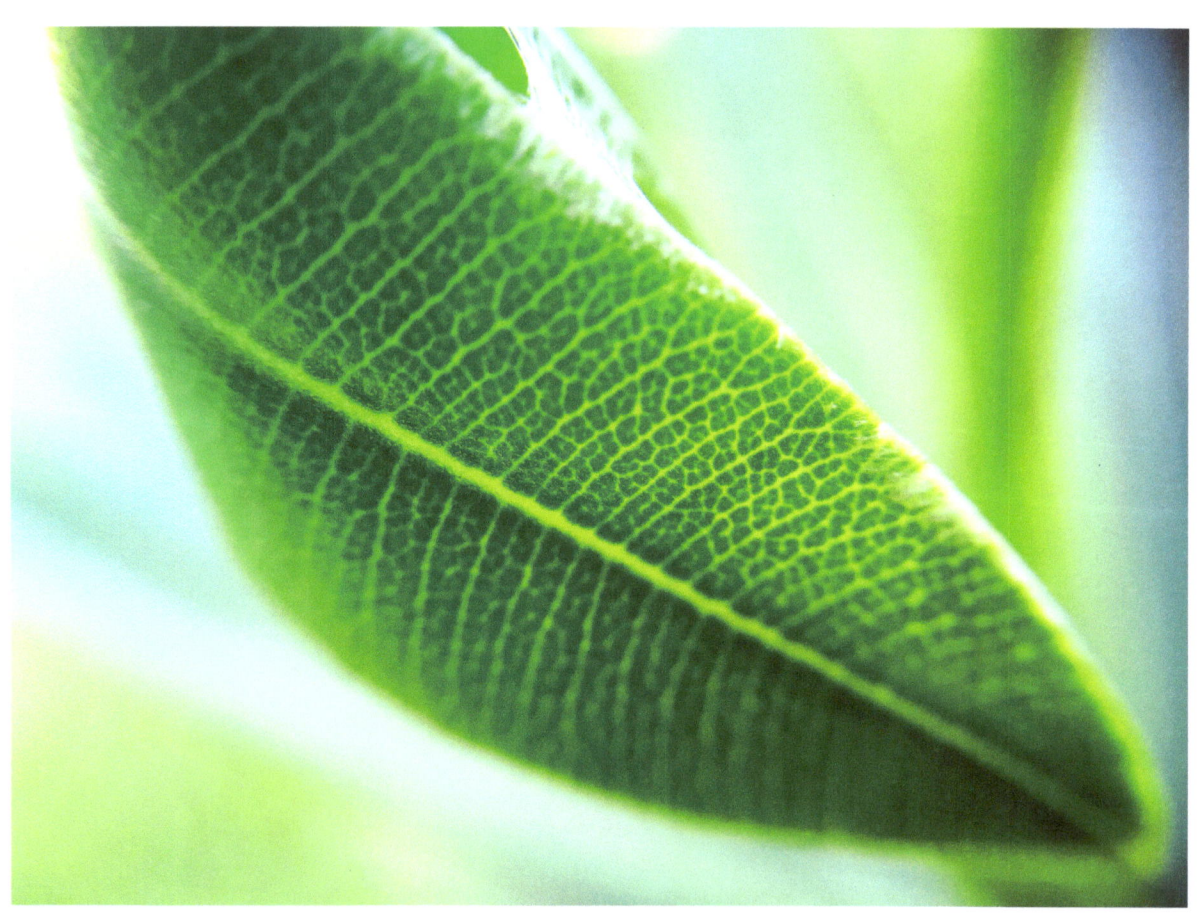

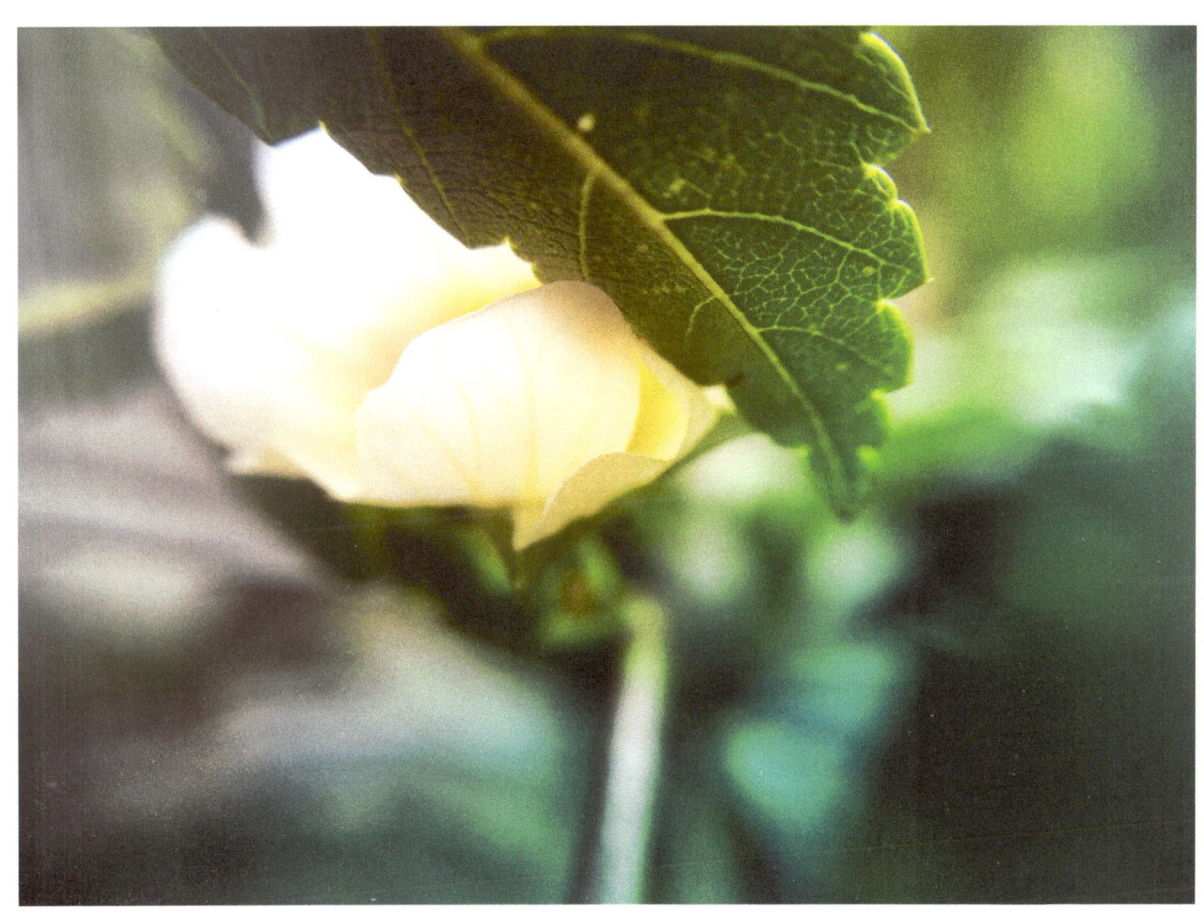

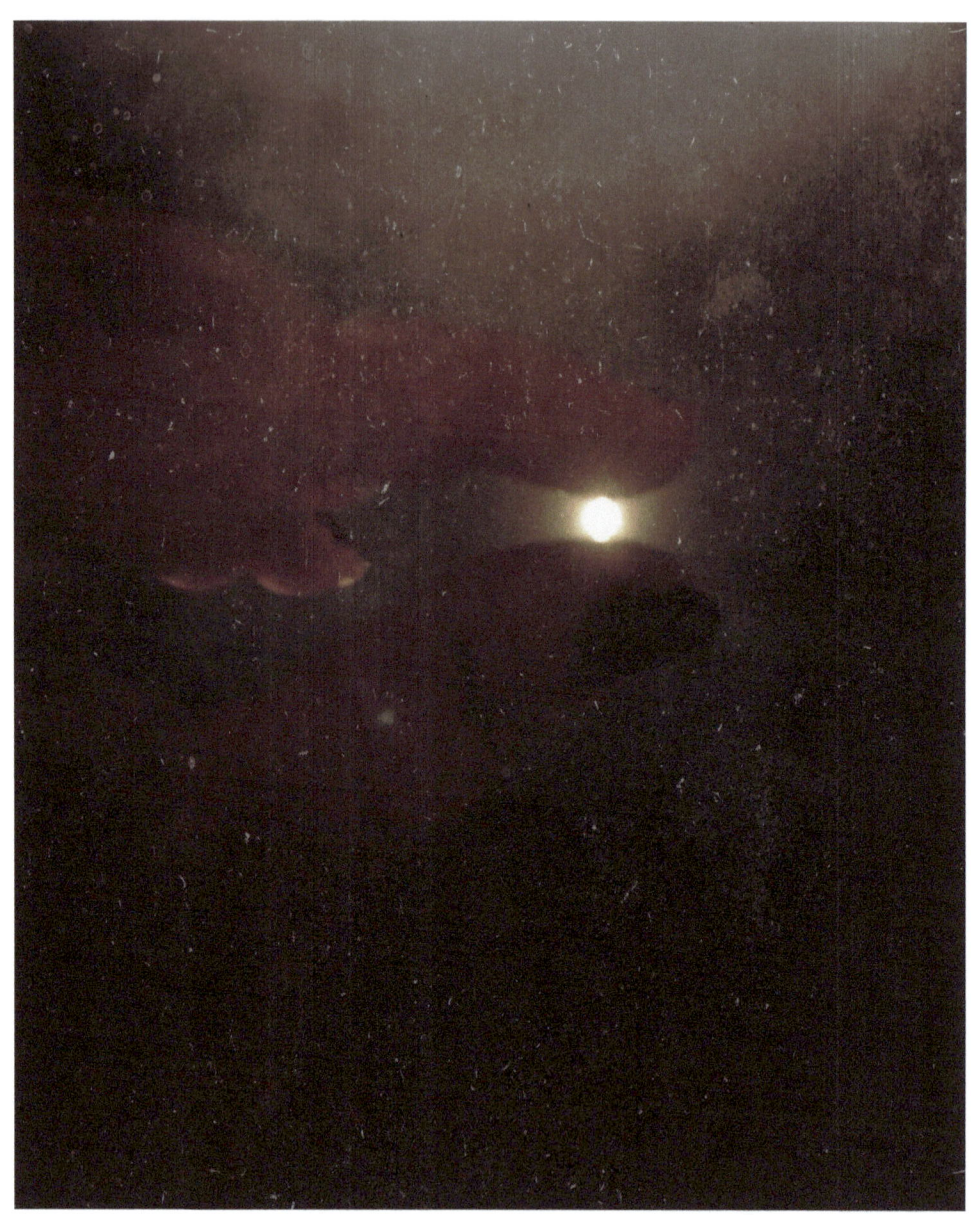

ABOUT THE ARTIST

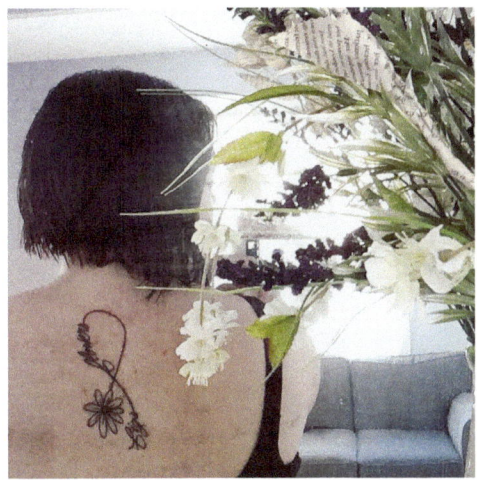

Starfleet graduate and mother of two pesky humanoid lifeforms. I dabble in writing, but my passion is photography. After my oldest broke my DSLR I decided that maybe expensive equipment wasn't for me, so I traded in my 'real equipment' for an iPhone.

I use macro lenses designed for phones for my macro work and I'm constantly learning from my mistakes.

All images are edited on the iPhone, first in Mextures, then through Instagram. Final edits are completed before printing, slight adjustments are made on a Mac only to improve the quality of the photo to print.

I enjoy what I do. I'm not looking for perfection, I believe flaws are a part of life and add beauty and truth to my images.

CONNECT
Instagram: @Chasingthewindphoto
Twitter: @ChasingTWphoto
Facebook: Chasing The Wind Photography